COLLINS PLAYS

You Made Me

by

Kelvin Reynolds
and
Adrian Lockwood

Series Consultant
Cecily O'Neill

Collins Educational

Published by Collins Educational, an imprint of HarperCollins*Publishers* Ltd, 77–85 Fulham Palace Road, London W6 8JB

© Copyright 2000 Kelvin Reynolds and Adrian Lockwood

First published 2000

ISBN 000 330 221 0

Kelvin Reynolds and Adrian Lockwood assert the moral right to be identified as the authors of the playscript.

All rights reserved. No part of this publication may be reproduced, stored in a retrieval system, or transmitted in any form or by any means, electronic, mechanical, photocopying, recording or otherwise, without either the prior permission of the Publisher or a licence permitting restricted copying in the United Kingdom issued by the Copyright Licensing Agency Ltd, 90 Tottenham Court Road, London W1P 9HE.

> Photocopying of scripts is illegal. Even if you hold a licence from the Copyright Licensing Agency, this only allows you to copy up to a total of 5% (i.e. one page in twenty) of the whole script.

British Library Cataloguing in Publication Data
A catalogue record for this book is available from the British Library.

Commissioned by Helen Clark, edited by Helen Clark and Angela Wigmore, picture research by Charles Evans

Cover design by Chi Leung, cover photograph reproduced courtesy of Sally & Richard Greenhill, internal design by Nigel Jordan

Whilst every effort has been made to contact the copyright holders, this has not proved possible in every case.

Production by Susan Cashin, printed and bound in Hong Kong

> For permission to perform this play, please allow plenty of time and contact:
> Permissions Department, HarperCollins*Publishers*,
> 77–85 Fulham Palace Road, London W6 8JB. Tel. 0181 741 7070.

Dedicated to Anna and Helena Johnson

Contents

PLAYSCRIPT

Characters   6

Playscript of *You Made Me*   7

RESOURCES

Staging the play   55

Work on and around the script   61

Themes in and around the play   68

Media   86

Resources   91

Acknowledgements   92

KEY

`71-74` `71-74`   cross-reference between playscript and teaching resources.

H   in resources = activity suitable for homework.

Characters

THE YOUNG PEOPLE

Kelly life about to change.
Lucy Kelly's annoying little sister.
Wayne the tough guy.
Leanne Wayne's rebellious sister.
Alan fighting all the aliens.
The Silent Child mysterious character who hardly speaks.
Chris Mr Northrop's stepson.

THE CHORUS

Up to six speaking parts, either in groups or as individuals – **Child One**, **Child Two**, etc.

THE ADULTS

Mr Ryan Kelly and Lucy's father.
Mrs Ryan Kelly and Lucy's mother.
Paul Mrs Ryan's new boyfriend.
Mr Snow Alan's father.
Mrs Snow Alan's mother.
Jane group counsellor.
Ros leading counsellor.
Mr Northrop Wayne's father.
Mrs Northrop Wayne's mother.
Jennie Mr Northrop's second wife.
Mr Gray Head of Year.
Mrs Golding School Principal.
The Judge
The Lawyer
Husband
Wife
Voice in Alan's Head

You Made Me

Scene One

The Breakdown

Sound of voices, one male, one female, arguing off-stage.

WIFE I'm just so fed up with it, day after day.

HUSBAND Wendy, will you please listen!

WIFE No, I'm sick of listening to you and your pathetic excuses.

HUSBAND Just stop shouting at me, will you? You'll wake Jade.

WIFE So you've noticed we've got a daughter then?

HUSBAND And what's that supposed to mean?

WIFE Well, you're never here for her.

HUSBAND Never here for her? That's because I'm working all day, slogging my guts out and paying for this house and this family –

WIFE Family? Family! Do you call this family life, Greg? This is just a joke.

HUSBAND Well, if you think you can do better somewhere else you know what you can do.

WIFE Yeah, well I might just do that!

HUSBAND I'm sick of all this.

WIFE Well, that makes two of us. *(fade out voice overs, music begins)*

Dance interpretation performed by members of cast. At the end of the dance five of the **Chorus** *members enter.*

Scene Two

Words

Child One Closer. Come closer. I've got something to tell you
and I don't want to shout. Listen. You must listen.
Words are important.
Other people's words can kill you, punch holes
through you like paper.
Sticks and stones may break my bones
but words will shatter me to pieces.

Child Two They went to war in 2004.
Mummy and Daddy are no more.

Child Three They went to war with words used as weapons.
Words used to destroy and rip each other apart.
In war there are casualties, it's to be expected.
My damage is inside me. It's built in. It's part
of the mechanism.

Child Four There was once a girl they called the Silent
Child. She oozed silence out of every pore and
her eyelids clamped shut like fists.
Blindness is revealing. Silence is golden.
Silence is precious; it can be broken.
Lock me in it. Let it embrace me.
Blast out the world with silence.
Let it drown the shouting, the breaking of glass,
the shattering of promises, the deadly trajectory
of accusations, the death scream of a family,
the detonation of a tear-drop.
Ssssh. Don't move. Don't flex a muscle.
Let there be stillness.
Let there be absolute silence.

Pause.

Chorus When the bough breaks, baby will fall
Down will come cradle, baby and all.

...and all...
...and all...

CHILD FIVE *(to audience)* You made me. Be careful. Handle with care.

Scene Three

Counselling

56, 59 *Waiting room.* **Kelly**, **Lucy, Alan** *and the* **Silent Child** *(who sits alone away from the others).* **Lucy** *plays with a board game.* **Kelly** *reads a magazine. Characters freeze.*

KELLY *(to audience)* I suppose it was like that for me. My own private war, played out inside my head as I took refuge under the covers. I couldn't always hear what they were arguing about, trivial things really, but it doesn't really matter. What did they get so angry about? I'd lie awake for ages wondering if they knew I could hear them, until it passed. And it always did. Then the All Clear came and… silence. It scared me at first, but I got used to it. And then the next day everything was back to normal again. But I was still shocked when they told me. Mum and Dad can't live together any more, they said… they didn't tell Lucy for ages, I suppose she was too young. I was older, I was responsible, I could handle it. But she kind of worked it out for herself. She's not stupid. And this is one of our compensations, a visit to the the Family Counselling unit every Thursday fortnight. Actually, this is a private one, we have to pay. But you can get free scholarships and assisted places. And so we sit here waiting. And waiting has become me. Waiting and never being at the place you want to be. Waiting to disintegrate. Or come together.

Lucy, **Alan** *and the* **Silent Child** *break freeze.*

LUCY Oh come on, let's have a game, pleeease.

KELLY Not now Lucy, stop bothering me.

LUCY You never want to play with me any more, nobody does.

KELLY That's not true.

LUCY Dad always played with me.

KELLY Well, he's not here, is he?

Lucy I shall tell him at the weekend. I shall tell him you're always picking on me. *(Kelly ignores Lucy)*

Lucy *(to Alan and the Silent Child)* Do you want a game?

Alan Uh… not really, not my game see. *(Silent Child stares)*

Lucy I suppose I'll just have to play on my own then!

Enter Wayne and Leanne.

Wayne *(to Alan)* How you doing, my main man! *(slaps Alan's palm)*

Alan Hiya, Wayne.

Wayne *(takes out cigarette)* You got a light, Alan?

Alan No, sorry.

Leanne 'Ere, bash us a fag.

Wayne Naff off, I ain't got any more.

Leanne Lying toe-rag. *(to Kelly)* Don't suppose you've got one?

Kelly I don't think you're allowed to smoke in here.

Leanne So?

Lucy You might get into trouble.

Wayne *(putting feet on table)* Big deal, I'm really scared. *(to Silent Child)* What you looking at, you ugly git?

Leanne Don't take any notice of him, he's just in a bad mood 'cos he got suspended from school.

Wayne Wasn't my fault, was it? Just 'cos I bunked off physics. You bunk off lessons and you get suspended and get more time off. Stupid, innit?

Leanne Oh come on, you did hit that kid in Year 8.

Wayne That was different, he was winding me up.

Leanne *(to Kelly)* I bet you're really clever, I bet you get 'A's for everything.

Kelly I don't, actually. My grades are down this term, I think my mum might get called in to see my Head of Year.

Leanne Huh. My mum wouldn't come up to the school, not just for a stupid grade. She don't give a monkey's, neither do I. It's all boring, anyway, but, like if there's any trouble, she's really supportive, you know. See 'cos there was this girl at school who was really slagging me off right? I sorted her out and I got detention for it, like it was my fault, right? And the teacher just blamed everything on to me and my mum says, 'Right you're not doing the detention 'cos you've gotta stand up for yourself and the teachers don't have the right to put you down for that'. So my mum came up and sorted her out, 'cos they've got no right to do that.

Kelly I suppose not.

Leanne See, it was the same with the social workers, 'cos they were going to put me and Wayne in care when my mum was ill, and they said we couldn't look after ourselves. I mean we are thirteen now and I'm not having no one telling me what to do.

Kelly So do you think they'll put you in care?

Leanne Dunno, do I? We went to a foster family once, only lasted three days. Wayne got totally smashed out of his head.

Wayne Yeah, it was wicked man! We drank all their cider.

Leanne Anyway, I got a sister in London and I could go and live with her if I want to.

Kelly What about… Do you have a dad?

Leanne Yeah! I do actually. He lives in Manchester, he would have us, but he's got this new baby like, and there's no room. Anyway, he's in Spain on holiday for two weeks. Only reason they want us to come here, social workers want to know all your business. Tell them nothing, right?

Lucy Our dad works in Sheffield. He makes computers. He's coming down this weekend, isn't he Kelly?

Alan I got an 'A' once. For a Geography project, on volcanoes.

WAYNE *(getting up)* Yeah, well I get 'A's for bunking off and messing about in class. *(approaches **Silent Child**)* Here, have you ever got totally smashed on cider? *(**Wayne** laughs – **Silent Child** doesn't respond)* Oi! I'm talking to you, Dumbo. Hello, this is England calling Planet Earth. Is there anyone at home? *(**Silent Child** ignores **Wayne**)*

KELLY I don't think that girl wants to talk to anyone.

WAYNE So what? I don't want to talk to her or anybody in this poxy place. Family therapy or whatever it's called, it's a waste of time. I've got my kick-boxing class at six. *(he demonstrates a few movements)*

LUCY What do they call it kick-boxing for? I thought you only used fists in boxing.

WAYNE What are you, stupid or something? It's martial arts, innit? My dad's been doing it for years, he's the area champion up north and he's gonna teach me proper like, so you lot better watch it.

LUCY *(to **Wayne**)* Do you want to play snakes and ladders?

WAYNE Oh yeah! *(he moves over to board)* I'll go first. *(shakes dice, moves counters up the board, then has another go)*

LUCY Hey you can't –

WAYNE Six and two, that's eight, up to the top, 100. I win.

LUCY That's not fair, you can't go up the snakes.

WAYNE I can do anything I like, anyway you gotta learn the snakes always win in this life.

KELLY Why don't you leave her alone, you big bully?

WAYNE Shut up.

LEANNE Yeah, shut up you prissy little tart.

WAYNE Here, if you want your poxy game, you can have it. *(throws board across room)*

Kelly You're so pathetic. *(confusion and shouting. Enter **Ros**, the group counsellor)*

Ros Ah, group dynamics, that's what I like to see, good communication, everyone getting to know everyone else. Hi everybody, I'm Ms Martin, but do call me Ros, because we're one big happy family here. My qualifications, a PhD in counselling and several articles in 'Dr Spock's Child Care Gazette' but I'm here to empathise, to share your pain, to understand your confrontational dilemmas, right? I know what you kids are going through, I feel your pain. And it's not your fault, because here at the centre we are not judgemental, OK? So just chill out and wear your heart on your sleeve. And say to yourself over and over again, I feel good, I feel so good about myself, it's so comforting, just let it go and remember you come through people not from them. Anyway, enough from me, I want to hear from you, I want to hear what you feel, I want to feel what you feel. Let's go for it. Would you like to begin? *(she approaches the **Silent Child**, who does not respond)* Yes, sometimes you feel bad about yourself and you have to say 'tomorrow is another day'. Sometimes it's tough and sometimes it gets better. So, what are we waiting for?

Scene Four

Wayne's World

*In **Wayne** and **Leanne's** home where they live with their mother. They are in the living room. **Leanne** is watching the TV while **Wayne** is pacing back and forth.*

WAYNE *(agitated)* When do you think he's going to arrive? It's already three o'clock.

LEANNE I don't know, do I? Look, why don't you just sit down and shut up for a second!

WAYNE Dad promised. He promised that we would have a kick-boxing session in the gym. He said so last night.

LEANNE Big deal. You can go anytime.

WAYNE Gym closes at half four. How long's it take to get from Manchester to here?

LEANNE I don't know! Stop asking me questions, you're getting on my bloomin' nerves, I'm trying to watch this! *(**Wayne** picks up the remote control and switches off the TV, then throws the remote out of the window)*

LEANNE Hey! What the… ?

WAYNE Don't ignore me, Leanne. Don't pretend I don't matter.

LEANNE You stupid prat! What are you playing at?!

WAYNE Got your attention, have I?

LEANNE Grow up Wayne. Stop playing the hurt little boy. You should know the routine by now. It's the same every time he comes, *when* he decides to give us his precious time, that is.

WAYNE Don't say that! He'll come. He said so on the phone last night, just you just watch.

LEANNE Yeah, yeah. I'll believe it when I see it.

Wayne Why can't you ever give him a break? He tries, I know he tries.

Leanne Come on Wayne, face it. You're not Daddy's favourite son any more, he's got two others now.

Wayne Shut up! Just shut up! How come he took *me* to the United game then, and not them? It was me he wanted to go with. Me.

Leanne Yeah, only because he blew you out the three times before that. I think even *our* father's got some sense of guilt. Takes some time before it kicks in though.

Wayne You always were Mummy's favourite. Like you cared when Dad moved out.

Leanne Good riddance, I say.

Wayne Yeah? And where's Mum now? At work? No. Out shopping? Nope. Surprise, surprise, she's in bed sick, *again*. Fat lot of use she is as a mother. We spend most of our time taking care of *her*.

Leanne Oh, you've really thought this one through haven't you! Whoa! Stand back, Wayne the Brain has had a thought! Too bad that the only original idea you've ever come up with is stupid!

Wayne I ought to smash your... Listen.

There is the sound of a car driving up to the house. The car horn sounds twice.

Wayne It's Dad. Won't come, huh? Eat your words dogface.

Mrs Northrop *(calling from off-stage)* Will one of you answer the door?

Wayne *(shouting up)* I'll get it. *(to himself)* Don't strain yourself, Mum.

Leanne I'll go see if Mum's all right while you tend to His Royal Highness. *(she goes upstairs)*

Wayne *opens the door. His father,* ***Mr Northrop,*** *is standing there with his stepson,* ***Chris****.* ***Wayne*** *is shocked. He can see* ***Jennie****, his father's new wife sitting in the car carrying their infant child.*

WAYNE *(to himself)* He's brought Jennie and the kids this time.

MR NORTHROP Well? Aren't you going to let us in? Come on, sport!

WAYNE Huh? Oh yeah. Sorry, Dad. Come in.

Scene Five
Passing Through

The Northrop's living room. **Wayne** *is sitting facing* **Mr Northrop** *who is on the couch with his stepson,* **Chris**.

WAYNE Isn't Jennie coming in? It might get cold outside in the car.

MR NORTHROP Uh, no. You know how it is with your mum.

WAYNE Oh, yeah. Do you want a drink, tea or something?

MR NORTHROP *You* make a cup of tea! Blimey! You really must want something!

WAYNE No, I just thought …

MR NORTHROP I'm kidding. What's happened to your sense of humour?! Your mother's seen to that too, has she? Look, we can't stay long anyway but I said I'd pop in to see how the two of you were doing.

WAYNE Oh, we're going soon are we?

MR NORTHROP We?

WAYNE Yeah. Remember what you said last night?

There is a silence from **Mr Northrop** *as he tries to remember.*

WAYNE *(hopelessly)* I guess kick-boxing can wait.

MR NORTHROP *(suddenly realising)* Oh yeah, kick-boxing. I hadn't forgotten. Really. It's just, you know, with the new baby and everything, we hardly get a chance to go out. Well, Jennie I mean. So I thought I'd take her to Westland, you know, the shopping mall. She loves that sort of thing, and so does Chris, don't yer, chuck? *(he ruffles* **Chris's** *hair. The boy laughs)* So listen mate, hope you don't mind. I mean, we'll do it, definitely, next time. I promise.

WAYNE *(crestfallen)* Yeah. Sure, no problem.

Leanne *and* ***Mrs Northrop*** *come down from upstairs.* ***Leanne*** *is supporting her mother who is still a bit giddy from her illness.*

MRS NORTHROP What's going on? Has someone died?

MR NORTHROP No, no. Everything's fine. You shouldn't have bothered coming down. I was just saying to **WAYNE** that we'd have to be going in a moment.

Mrs Northrop *notices* ***Chris*** *for the first time. She glances out of the window and sees* ***Jennie*** *sitting in the car. She turns and stares at her ex-husband.*

MRS NORTHROP *(to Mr Northrop)* You've brought Jennie and the kids… I need to talk to you for a minute.

Scene Six

Piggy in the Middle

Kelly *is packing her bag.* **Lucy** *tries to remove the headphones on the table from the personal stereo.*

Kelly Hey, leave them alone. *(snatching them back)*

Lucy These are mine, look they've got a blue mark on.

Kelly You've broken yours, you know you have.

Lucy Give them back now! *(***Lucy** *tries to pull them away, but* **Kelly** *puts them in her bag)*

Kelly *(triumphantly)* They're mine.

Lucy I hate you!

Kelly Just go away will you?

Lucy It's not fair. You've already got two pairs, and I haven't got any. *(***Lucy** *storms off)*

Kelly *(to audience)* Little sisters, such a pain. But she's right, of course. I have got two personal stereos. In fact, I've got two of just about everything. That's what happens, you see, you get two lots of birthday presents, two lots of Christmas presents, two holidays and two homes. At first, it's quite exciting, but now I'm fed up with it. *(sighs as she packs)* Every weekend it's the same, it's so tedious. I want to go out with my friends and enjoy myself, but then I wouldn't get to see Dad. I hate all this packing up, just for a day, and then you have to unpack it all again when you get home on Sunday. It's so time-consuming. What shall I wear? The black top? Or the white top? No, stick to a shade of grey. It makes life easier. It's all so confusing, I change my opinions all the time to fit in. Agreeing with one side, and then the other. Being careful not to criticise or hurt their feelings. It's so difficult trying to please everyone all the time. Funny, they can't live with each other, but they have to know every little detail about what the other one's doing. I feel like the Internet – access to all information. They stopped firing the missiles a long time ago. Hostilities were replaced by mutual suspicion. Now it's the age of the cold war, the uneasy peace and I'm in no man's land, trapped on the barbed wire, like piggy in the middle.

Scene Seven
Packing

Chorus Table of contents:
   I've got the toothbrush
   so the rot doesn't set in.
   I've got my pictures and poems
   swelling with my secrets in.
   I've got my old walking shoes,
   to get me there and back again,
   there and back, there and back.
   Tick-tock, tick-tock.
   I've got my heavy boots for the driving rain,
   and a stereo sound that can drown out the pain.
   I've got my return ticket for the Inter-rail,
   a broken teddy from the jumble sale.
   Mummy's waiting by the bus bay,
   be back to Dad by Saturday.
   Mummy's on the inside,
   Daddy's on the outside,
   I'm by the wayside –
   piggy in the middle,
   piggy in the middle.
   She's so little,
   she's so brittle.
   Time to go,
   time to come,
   Time to stand,
   time to run.

Scene Eight
The Commander

*Alan's home. **Alan** is sitting on the stairs with his electronic game. **Alan** lives with his mother. His father has just brought him home about half an hour later than the arranged time. Downstairs, **Alan's** parents, **Mr Snow** and **Mrs Snow**, are arguing in hushed tones so that **Alan** won't hear.*

MRS SNOW *(quietly)* So, you couldn't even do this right, get him home on time. You can't just do whatever you want with him. I've been worried, worried sick. I almost called the police. I should have known it was just your lack of organisation.

MR SNOW It was heavy traffic.

MRS SNOW Well, you should have left earlier. You know he gets upset if he doesn't follow his routine. I'll be dealing with this for days now. God knows what you've done to him. I don't know why I ever married you in the first place. I needed a man and I got you instead.

MR SNOW *(trying to contain his anger)* He's fine. He was chatty in the car.

MRS SNOW Oh well then, how wonderful that *you've* had such a good time and I'm left to pick up the pieces. I hope you can live with yourself. You call yourself a man. You can't do anything without messing it up.

MR SNOW Fine. I'll call the lawyers tomorrow if that's what you want.

MRS SNOW Well, maybe it's time we resolved this once and for all…

*The argument goes on. **Alan** hears every word. He switches on his electronic game.*

ALAN *(to himself)* Forget it, father. You will never win. But I will. *(in super-hero type voice)* I, Alan Snow, Commander of the Elite Defence Force, will repel the invading alien hoards that have planned to destroy our planet – a lonely planet called… Earth.

*Alan begins playing his game, zapping aliens with ferocity. The **Voice** in **Alan's** head begins to speak.*

Voice Does Commander Alan Snow of Earth's Elite Defence Force always wet his pants at school?

Alan *(his space-craft is destroyed by a barrage of enemy laser fire)* Ugh! You made me lose my concentration.

Voice Oh dear, oh dear. You're not having a very successful day, are you? First you lose control of your bladder during a Geography lesson, then you allow the Earth to be vaporised because of my little voice.

Alan I'd rather not talk about the Geography incident. In fact, I'd much rather forget it.

Voice Just because you got an 'A' in a Geography project on volcanoes doesn't mean you have the right to go peeing all over the floor. What were you thinking? You weren't doing anything on flooding at the time, were you?

Alan Very funny. It was an accident. Anyway, why can't you leave me alone? You turn up at the most inconvenient times.

Voice Are you saying you don't want me around?

Alan Yes. Go and find something high to jump off!

Voice Now, now. That's not very nice is it? Mother taught you never to speak to people like that, and you know you must always do as Mother says, like not peeing in your pants in public. Ooops! Sorry. Didn't mean to bring it up again.

Alan Just go away! I'm tired of talking to you.

Voice But who else would you talk to? It's not like you have any friends, is it? You're not exactly Mr Popular at school are you?

Alan Well… there's that girl. You know, the one that doesn't say much.

Voice Oh yes, the Silent Child. That fruit-cake from the counselling group. Wow! What a find!

Alan She's OK.

Voice What's her name, then?

Alan Uh, I, er, can't remember.

Voice You mean, you don't even know, do you?! And you know why? Because she's never said a word to you, or anybody. I bet your conversations together are a real blast!

Alan Look, she's just a bit mixed up at the moment. She's living in a foster home and it's not easy. Her baby brother died last year. It got too much and that's why her parents split up. At least I know that much.

Voice Oh, you're *soooo* caring. But face it, Commander Alan, the kid's nuttier than a squirrel's back yard.

Alan Probably just needs someone.

Voice My dear boy, let's talk man to man. It is my humble belief that it is *you* who needs someone. Come on now, it's true isn't it? Poor little Alan, all alone. And by the way, that silent kid is not the only fruit-cake around here; why do you insist on calling yourself Commander Alan when you are just a little boy that widdles in his trousers?

Alan *(covering his ears)* Go away, just get lost!!

Voice Oh bother, here comes mummy. I better go away before she finds you talking to yourself. We don't want anybody else knowing you're mad, do we? Speak to you later Commander Widdle.

*The **Voice** fades away. **Mrs Snow** comes up the stairs.*

Mrs Snow What on earth were you shouting at? *(Alan doesn't reply)* Never mind. You better come down and say goodbye to your father; you may not be seeing him for some time. Then, young man, I want to talk about what happened in Geography today. As if I haven't got enough to worry about.

Alan Yes, mother. *(Mrs Snow exits)* Stardate twenty-ninety-nine. Home life is like science fiction and I'm watching the two biggest planets preparing for cold war. They build up their defences like body armour and razor sharp steel. Sometimes their voices don't touch each other and their eyes don't fall on one another. Nobody says a word. The world erupts but the surface stays calm. Then sometimes the whole world screams and shatters.

Scene Nine
A. W. O. L.

*The Head of Year's office at **Alan's** school. The Year Head, **Mr Gray**, is sitting at his desk. In front of him are **Alan** and **Mrs Snow**.*

MR GRAY Urinating in his trousers in a Geography lesson, locking himself in the stock cupboard, hiding alone under the Science block stairs at lunchtimes. Mrs Snow, we are more than a little worried about Alan's unusual behaviour, which has changed considerably in the last six months.

MRS SNOW Well, I don't know what it can be. He's such a good boy at home. Always very quiet, does his homework and never makes a fuss. In fact, sometimes you wouldn't even know he was there.

MR GRAY Actually, Mrs Snow, that's part of the problem – he barely ever talks, to anybody, except himself of course.

MRS SNOW Are you suggesting that my son is going mad?

MR GRAY No, I'm not. But I do think that something outside school is making him behave in this way.

MRS SNOW You're saying that it's my fault, that I'm responsible.

MR GRAY No, Mrs Snow, it's not as straightforward as that. Now, I'm aware that you and your husband are having, er… marital difficulties at the moment.

MRS SNOW How dare you talk about my private life! What right do you have to interfere in my affairs?

MR GRAY Please calm down, Mrs Snow. All I'm suggesting is that perhaps the situation at home is affecting Alan in a way that you wouldn't expect.

MRS SNOW Are you a psychologist, Mr Gray?

MR GRAY No… no, I'm not.

Mrs Snow Are you a social worker, then?

Mr Gray No. But what I'm trying to say is…

Mrs Snow *(interrupting)* Then keep your nose out of my business. And just for your information, Alan has been going to a private counselling group, at considerable expense to myself. The therapist has taught him how to deal with the home situation perfectly adequately.

Mrs Snow stands up, gathers her coat and handbag and walks out. **Alan** *quietly follows her. When they are a good distance away from the office,* **Mrs Snow** *turns to her son.*

Mrs Snow *(to* **Alan***)* Don't you dare ever humiliate me like that again, do you understand? *(***Alan** *makes no reply but looks at the ground.* **Mrs Snow** *raises her voice)*

Mrs Snow Do you understand?!

Alan Yes, mother.

Mrs Snow walks off to the car. **Alan** *is left behind. He slowly makes his way to class, stops, turns around and crawls under a stairwell to hide.*

Scene Ten

Battleground

Mr and Mrs Northrop are in the kitchen out of ear-shot of Wayne and Leanne.

MR NORTHROP OK, what is it now? *(sarcastically)* What has bad ol' Daddy done now?

MRS NORTHROP You sod.

MR NORTHROP Oh, come on. I'm sure he'll survive. He's a tough lad is Wayne.

MRS NORTHROP Yes, no bloody thanks to you!

MR NORTHROP Look, I'm going. I don't need this. This is exactly what drove me out of here in the first place.

MRS NORTHROP *(sarcastically)* What's that, then? You mean responsibility? Being there for your kids? That's what drove you away?

MR NORTHROP No. Just you.

MRS NORTHROP Forget me. But couldn't you just this one time have kept a promise to your son? He's your first son.

MR NORTHROP It's no big deal. We'll do it next time. Wayne's not even bothered. He said it was fine. It's only you trying to stir it all up again. You don't need to do that, we're not married any more, in case you hadn't noticed.

MRS NORTHROP He's putting on a brave face, don't you get it? Being tough, trying to be a man, like his father once taught him a long time ago.

MR NORTHROP Oh, please.

MRS NORTHROP He's waited all month for this. He's always waiting, waiting for you.

MR NORTHROP Look Sue, it's getting late. I have to go.

Mrs Northrop Sometimes I could just hate you.

Mr Northrop Look, I'll make it up to him. I promise.

Mrs Northrop Yeah. You do that.

Mr Northrop exits.

Scene Eleven
Fall Out

*Wayne's bedroom. **Wayne** is sitting at a desk looking out of the window. It is starting to rain outside. There is a gentle knock on the door and **Leanne** enters.*

LEANNE Dad's gone then… has he?

WAYNE *(still looking outside)* Really Leanne?! I'm so glad that I've got such an amazingly intelligent sister to tell me the most obvious things! By the way, I don't remember saying you could come in here so you can just leave right now.

LEANNE Look Wayne, I know how you feel…

WAYNE *(turning around)* Oh, really? You know what it feels like to be made a complete fool of by your own father? You know what it's like to always lie to yourself that things will be different the next time, when inside you know that nothing will change?

LEANNE No, I just wanted to see how you were.

WAYNE Come to say I told you so I expect.

LEANNE You're just so full of it, Wayne! He's my father too. Did you forget that? *(**Wayne doesn't** answer but turns and looks out of the window again)* Wayne, it's me you're talking to. You don't need to do the tough guy routine, you're not in counselling or school now.

WAYNE *(softly)* I just feel so stupid. I should have known. I'm always stupid.

LEANNE Hey, don't flatter yourself. I've been suspended from school too, you know.

WAYNE Yeah, but when you get suspended you do it brilliantly. You stand up for yourself and argue your point so well that the Principal throws you out because she's too thick to know what to say to you. When I get chucked out it's because I do dumb things, like hitting that Year 8 kid.

Leanne He did call you a brain-dead gorilla.

Wayne But do you know why I hit him? Because I knew he was right. I lumber around trying to look tough so everyone will leave me alone and not see that I'm just some stupid kid who wants his dad. Funny, the only person I really feel like hitting is Dad.

Leanne Get used to it. Dad's gone. He's not coming back.

Wayne What's the point in trying to be good, trying your hardest and everything. He doesn't care so why should I? I've got nothing to lose now.

Leanne You can't go on with that attitude.

Wayne Oh yeah?! Well, who's gonna stop me?

Leanne How's anything going to get better?

Wayne Oh shut up, Leanne. Nothing's ever going to get better and neither am I. Now get out of my room.

Leanne Oh come on, Wayne.

Wayne *(shouting)* Just get out!

Leanne sighs and reluctantly leaves Wayne to his anger.

Scene Twelve
Zoo Time

Kelly and *Lucy* are at the zoo.

Kelly *(to audience)* If it's Saturday, it must be zoo time. I know them all: London, Chester, Norfolk, Whipsnade. Actually, they're not all called zoos. Sometimes they're called nature parks or animal sanctuaries but it all amounts to the same thing. They're our sanctuaries, really. You can spot us on any weekend, whole armies of kids on the move, with their away-day passes and season tickets. The zoo, the last place of refuge for the dysfunctional family. No wonder animals are so popular.

Kelly and *Lucy* approach the monkeys' cage.

Lucy Oh, look! That poor little one hasn't got anything to eat and I haven't got any peanuts left.

Kelly They're not playing with him, he's all on his own.

Lucy Perhaps he's not very well.

Kelly He might be one of those rejected ones, they do that sometimes. The rest just ignore him, that's probably why he's on his own.

Lucy But why? He hasn't done anything… It's not fair.

Kelly That's nature I suppose. Oh, look! That one's got a little baby.

Lucy Where?

Kelly At the back, look, the mother's feeding it.

Lucy Oh, he's so sweet. I wish I could take him home.

Kelly Yeah, the trouble is they don't stay babies forever.

Scene Thirteen
Long Division

Mr Ryan and Mrs Ryan sit facing each other dividing up their possessions. They speak coldly, in an unemotional style.

MR RYAN Cutlery set?

MRS RYAN Mine.

MR RYAN Kitchen stools?

MRS RYAN You can have them.

MR RYAN Right. Carriage clock?

MRS RYAN Yours.

MR RYAN But that was a present from my mother.

MRS RYAN All the more reason for you to have it.

MR RYAN But I thought you liked it.

MRS RYAN I think it's hideous, I never have liked it.

MR RYAN Oh, all right. *(picking up records)* Can I have The Beatles LP?

MRS RYAN OK. What about all that stuff in the attic?

MR RYAN Dunno. Advertise it. Car boot sale, perhaps?

MRS RYAN Put it one of those free papers.

MR RYAN Now then, garden chairs and table.

MRS RYAN Yours.

MR RYAN Ornamental frogs and gnomes.

MRS RYAN Mine.

Lucy enters between her Mr and Mrs Ryan and sits down amongst their possessions. The couple freeze in position, only Lucy speaks.

Lucy Situation vacant.
One child, house-trained,
bargain basement, prospects bleak –
free to a good home every Saturday week.
Two careful owners, good experience of life:
a ping-pong ball for husband and wife.
Legal enforcements, access denied.
No-blame situation, so who's taking sides?
First it's the clock, then the Beatles LP,
sooner or later, they'll get round to me.

Scene Fourteen
Dishonourable Discharge

*Alan's bedroom. He has been grounded for playing truant under the stairs at school. **Alan** is sitting on his bed leaning against the wall.*

ALAN *(to himself)* Stardate twenty-three-ninety-nine. Here sits *ex-*Commander Alan Snow of Earth's Elite Defence Forces in a dingy cavern in hostile alien territory. He is stripped of his rank, disgraced before all, and charged with betraying Earth to the enemy. It's sometimes difficult to do the right thing when you don't know who the enemy is. Sometimes they are the people closest to you.

*The **Voice** in **Alan's** head wakes up.*

VOICE Well, fancy meeting you here! Who's a grumpy boy, then?

ALAN Oh no! Just go away. The last thing I need is you!

VOICE Oh come, come. You make it sound as if you want to be alone.

ALAN Well, I do actually. Just get lost!

VOICE My dear boy, I can help. Just tell me what the problem is.

ALAN How can you help? You're just a voice that comes out of *my* head. If I don't know what to do, how can you, an annoying, pompous, disembodied blabbermouth, possibly have a clue about what's going on?!!

VOICE Tut, tut, tut. My, my. Such aggression. Such anger. We have a lot of work to do on you. Now, my irritable little friend, it might come as a surprise to you, but I do have access to all sorts of interesting files that you've forgotten about here in this teeny-weeny peanut-sized thing you call a mind. Who knows, they may come in handy.

Alan Great! As if I don't have enough problems! Now I've got some psychopathic banana brain with a big mouth rooting around in my head!

Voice Hey buddy, don't forget that I'm part of you – if I'm mad then you're a nutcase too, but we knew that anyway didn't we? Besides, I think you're just afraid.

Alan Afraid of what?

Voice Everything.

Alan Shut up!

Voice Oooh! I'm sooooo scared, please don't hurt me! Touched a nerve, didn't I?

Alan No.

Voice Wanna bet? *(Alan is silent)* Hey Al, listen to me. There's nothing wrong with being afraid.

Alan I am Commander Alan, Earth's only hope. I can't be afraid. The slightest sign of fear and I will be destroyed.

Voice Oh boy, is this going to be a long day! Look Commander Alan, time for a reality check. You dig, brother?

Alan Oh, brilliant. Now he's a hippy!

Voice You could travel a thousand galaxies a billion light-years away; you could destroy the evil galactic forces of the planet Wibbleblop a hundred times over, but you can never run away from yourself. However, you're so stupid, you just keep trying to run. What's the point of running if you've got nowhere to go?

Alan But Mum and Dad both say that I should be strong, like them, that it isn't easy for anyone at the moment.

Voice Oh boy! Adults! Can't live with them and you can't put them in a blender! Listen Al, my pal, you've got to deal with it in your own way. You've got to be brave to allow yourself to be scared. Don't you know, most adults spend their lives being afraid of things. It's only natural. Anyway, I've said my piece. I'm going to check out now, beam up, or whatever crazy thing it is you do. Just think about what I've said.

ALAN Yeah thanks, whatever your name is. *(the **Voice** disappears. **Alan** is silent and thoughtful)*

ALAN The world's running weird and my craft is spinning out of control in the intergalactic darkness. This isn't supposed to happen to the Commander of Earth's Elite Defence Forces. What's wrong with me? Where's my cool gone? I'm meant to keep a level head under heavy enemy fire. I've been trained not to break under pressure. But here I am breaking. Falling apart in a most unheroic manner. Maybe I was never cut out to be Commander after all. Perhaps I'm the alien instead. The truth is out there, but where am I? What am I to do now that my navigation's gone? Space is a cold place. I need to be brought back in. Mum, Dad – you need to love the alien.

Scene Fifteen
Silent Scream

*The **Silent Child** is sitting on a chair opposite her counsellor, **Jane**.*

JANE I know you're frightened. We're here to help you. *(the **Silent Child** looks away from her)*

JANE I know that this must be awful for you. You don't need to speak straight away if you don't feel like it. It is OK to be frightened. Just talk when you're ready. *(the **Silent Child** raises her eyes slightly to look at **Jane** then lowers them again)* When my parents separated, I felt abandoned. It took me a long time before I could start to speak about it.

*There is a silence between the two. **Jane** allows the silence to continue for some time.*

JANE You must be feeling confused. One of the things that I'm here to do is help you to see what you're really feeling and accept what you feel. Feelings are funny things, aren't they? You might think that you're perfectly OK but when you look closely enough you might see that, really, you're falling to bits. Don't feel guilty about your emotions.

*The **Silent Child** begins to drift off into a day-dream. **Jane's** voice becomes an echo: 'Don't feel guilty... Don't feel guilty...' In the dream the **Silent Child** is in a large, empty room. The ceiling seems to hang miles above her and the walls are dark grey. In the middle of the room there is a towering pulpit. Behind it sits a dark, hunched figure in the robes and wig of a **Judge**.*

JUDGE Where is the accused? Bring in the miserable wretch!

*Footsteps echo from behind the **Silent Child**. Enter the **Lawyer**, a woman in black robes with a pale, white face.*

LAWYER Yes, Your Honour. *(leads the **Silent Child** forward to the foot of the pulpit)*

Silent Child Why am I here? What is this place?

Judge Welcome to your nightmare, toad. You have brought yourself here. This is a place that you have made. We are the disciples of your twisted mind.

Silent Child If you are just in my head, then I order you to go away!

Judge *(laughing menacingly)* You don't get away that easily, wretch! We like it here. We're going to stay. Counsel, read out the accusations made against this... this crumpled specimen of humanity.

Lawyer Yes, Your Honour. The following accusations have been made against the prisoner for crimes against the family: failure to comprehend the true significance of the parental rift before it was too late; failure to prevent the break up of the family; failure to communicate a preference for one or the other parent; failure to... Your Honour, I could go on, but this endless list clearly indicates the prisoner's unforgivable failure to resolve the domestic situation in a time of marital crisis.

Silent Child Who has brought these charges against me?

Judge *(shaking)* SILENCE, you morsel! You don't seem to understand – you have brought these charges against yourself. You are the accused and the accuser. Be clear about this, you remnant. Counsel, proceed.

Lawyer Certainly Your Honour. *(turning to the **Silent Child**)* Now, what is your defence?

Silent Child Defence? I hadn't thought... I have none.

Lawyer Have none? Surely you have a carefully formulated plan to deflect these accusations?

Silent Child *(shouting)* What could I have done?

Judge *(banging gavel furiously)* SILENCE! Another outburst like that and you will be held in contempt!

Lawyer Is it not true that in the period between August 2005 and January 2008 you failed to recognise the signs of a deteriorating marriage and thus to take preventative measures?

Silent Child What? I...

Lawyer Answer me this, then. Was it not obvious from the strained silences when you were around, the fury of voices that crept through the floor-boards from downstairs when you were supposed to be in bed, the frequently tear-stained eyes of your mother?

Silent Child I saw it, but what could I do? What could I do?

Lawyer How did crying alone in your bed help anything? How did hiding the pain from those around you make things better? How did not speaking out help the situation? Why don't you answer these questions?

Silent Child *(quietly)* I can't. Because I can't...

Judge It would appear that the evidence before the court is incontrovertible. Never in my entire life have I seen such a blatant case of utter ineptitude. So, worm, you will suffer the full penalty of your conscience. You have been found... GUILTY!

*The **Judge** and the **Lawyer** seem to dissolve into the air.*

Silent Child I have been powerless. I have been useless. This should not be a child's world. This shouldn't have happened to me. I should be out there, dancing in the music of sunlight, inventing secrets with friends, growing, seeing, being alive. But I am in this place, a place that Mummy and Daddy have constructed for me to live in. I am alone here. It shouldn't be like this. They made me, but left me undone. They made me and sometimes I want to be unmade... unmade... unmade. *(the **Silent Child** comes out of the day-dream with a slight start. The room is quiet. The sun shines through the window)*

Scene Sixteen
First Contact

*Alan and the **Silent Child** have just finished a counselling group meeting. They are waiting outside to be picked up.*

ALAN *(messing about to pass the time by timing how long he can hold his breath. His eyes look as if they are about to pop out and he suddenly exhales)* Blaaaah! Boy that was dumb! *(the **Silent Child** glances at **Alan**)* It wasn't that funny! I could have suffocated, or worse still, air bubbles could have gone to my brain and I would have needed micro brain surgery to sort the whole mess out. Except, the only surgeon that can do it has been abducted by aliens who need him to mutate human embryos for their eventual invasion of the Earth. *(the **Silent Child** looks at him puzzled)* Forget it. You wouldn't understand. So, er, what's your opinion on the government conspiracy to cover up the existence of extra-terrestrial life? *(the **Silent Child** turns away shyly now that Alan is speaking directly to her)* You don't say much, do you? I guess some people just don't want to talk. Look, if I tell you something, will you promise not to laugh? *(the **Silent Child** glances at him, looking intrigued)* Well, you see, I've got this person that talks to me. Well, actually, it's not really a person, more like a voice… in my head. Not any ordinary voice. I can't really control it and it won't listen when I tell it to go away. *(**Alan** checks to see if the **Silent Child** is still listening. She looks interested so he carries on)* I think I'm losing it, going crackers, potty, barmy. *(the **Silent Child** looks away)* Oh, don't worry, I'm not dangerous or anything, just a bit mixed up. I've got this idea, right. Maybe, just maybe it could be an alien implant. You know, a mind control device. I could be some kind of specimen in an alien experiment. It's probably all part of their fiendish plan. Once they've sapped my brain dry they will take over my body, and… *(the **Silent Child** looks at him, puzzled)* Sorry. I sometimes get carried away. You know what? I think I'm going to give my voice a name. I know, I'll give him a girl's name – that'll teach him. I'll call him Mary, as in 'Mary, Mary quite contrary' on account of him never doing what I say. *(shouting)* Hey 'Voice'. Yeah, you in my head. Do you hear that? I know you're there somewhere. *(the **Silent Child** stares at **Alan** then looks* *away trying to hide a smile)* Sorry. But you see what he does to me? He makes me look like I'm mad… maybe I am. *(the **Silent Child** looks at him in a comforting way)* I've… I've been wondering lately where things went wrong for me. There was a time when I was happy… I think. A time before the voice started in my head. Mum and Dad used to take me to the park. They'd both wait to catch me at the bottom of the slide. Now, it's like I'm sliding into this great big, gaping black hole, and there's no one waiting to catch me at the bottom. It could be that I'm just a coward. *(**Alan** is startled when the **Silent Child** touches his hand to comfort him)* Hey… thanks. I didn't mean to jump. I guess things must be bad for you too, huh? *(the **Silent Child** lets go of his hand and doesn't answer)* It's OK. You don't have to say anything. But you know, we're only kids. Maybe we're supposed to be afraid. If we weren't then we'd be mad. Funny, the Voice once said something like that to me. Mum is always saying to me that I've got to be strong, that I've got to be a man and stand up to all these things, but I just can't. Adults are always telling children to do things that they sometimes can't do themselves. It's like they think it's their duty, or something. They're scared most of the time, too. Hey, that's a thought! Actually, that Voice with the big brains, and big mouth told me that too. I suppose if he's going to live in my head, he ought to be of some use. Maybe I should try listening to him more. *(a car pulls into the big drive and the **Silent Child** picks up a bag)* Hey look, er, thanks. Thanks for listening. I don't know your name or anything, but it helped, you know, talking about it. *(the **Silent Child** gives a slight wave then hurries to the car. On the way, she turns around and mouths something to Alan)* Hey! Wait. I didn't hear what you said… too late. Oh, well.

*The **Voice** in **Alan's** head wakes up.*

Voice Hey, Commander Bird-brain. I heard what you said.

Alan Oh yeah? About what?

Voice About listening to me more. Go on. Admit it. You said it.

Alan Maybe I did, maybe I didn't.

Voice Well, you won't be hearing from me for much longer.

Alan *(surprised)* What? Why? Where are you going?

Voice Going to miss me?

Alan No! Of course not. I just pity the next kid whose head you get into. Why *are* you leaving, by the way?

Voice Well, perhaps you've started to find your own way. You won't need me to keep bugging you any more. Uh-oh. Someone's coming. I'd better go before they find you talking to yourself and have you locked up. Still, wouldn't be such a bad idea. Oh, by the way, I resent that gag about the name – Mary doesn't suit me at all. I'm far more sophisticated than a common Mary.

Alan Yeah, yeah. All right. Shut up will you!

Voice Well, best be going. Toodle-oo. Take care of yourself, Commander Alan and take it easy on those extra-terrestrials. Aliens need love too you know. *(silence)*

Alan Well, that's that, I guess. Now where's Dad?

Scene Seventeen
The Storming

*Wayne is sitting in the Principal's office. He is looking sullen and has his arms crossed over his chest. He doesn't look the Principal, **Mrs Golding**, in the eye.*

Mrs Golding Violence is not the answer, Wayne. You should know that by now. Have you got anything to say? *(**Wayne** is silent and stares at the floor)* The boy was only in Year 8, Wayne. Do you know how much bigger you are than he is?

Wayne He was bugging me.

Mrs Golding I'm sure that he was, but there are other ways of dealing with that kind of situation.

Wayne I can't do anything right, can I?

Mrs Golding Well, that's really up to you, Wayne.

Wayne Well, are you going to expel me or not?

Mrs Golding No, Wayne. You've got one more chance. You'll be suspended for a week. But all it will take is one more assault on another pupil.

Wayne Can I go now?

Mrs Golding With that attitude, Wayne, you won't last here much longer will you?

Wayne *(sarcastically)* Can I go now, please?

Mrs Golding I think you had better. Your father is waiting outside. Please send him in, I will need to talk to him before you both leave. *(**Wayne** exits)*

*Later in the car as **Mr Northrop** drives **Wayne** home.*

Mr Northrop I can't understand why you keep doing this.

Wayne You don't understand anything.

Mr Northrop Now come on Wayne, that's not fair.

Wayne Oh, it isn't fair, is it? What about you letting me down all the time? How fair is that?

Mr Northrop Well, don't I make it up to you in the end?

Wayne It's too late by then, Dad. I'm sick of being your second thought.

Mr Northrop *(speaking severely now)* You listen to me, lad. You better start bucking up your ideas or there's going to be real trouble coming your way.

Wayne Oh yeah, what are you going to do? Come down all the way from Manchester again to give me a spanking? Nobody's going to stop me doing what I do. Nobody does anything for me, so why should I put myself out for them?

Mr Northrop Wayne.

Wayne Go on, try doing something. Let's see how far you get. I've done listening to everyone talk about how I should behave. But what about you, all you responsible adults? What about how you should behave? All I've ever seen from you and Mum has been anger and disappointment. Anger. That's all I know now, Dad. That's all I've got to get me through. There's nothing else there for me.

The car stops at a traffic light. **Wayne** *opens the door and gets out.*

Mr Northrop Wayne, get back in! Come on, get in the car!

Wayne Forget it Dad, I'll walk. I'll make my own way.

Wayne walks off into the crowded street before **Mr Northrop** *can stop him.*

46

Scene Eighteen
My Mum's New Boyfriend

Mrs Ryan enters with her friend, Paul, who is about to be introduced to Kelly and Lucy for the first time.

MRS RYAN This is Kelly, my eldest, and this is Lucy.

LUCY Hi! *(Kelly says nothing)*

PAUL Pleased to meet you, girls. *(noticing printed T-shirt worn by Lucy)* Who's that then? One of the Spice Girls?

LUCY *(laughing)* No! It's Britney Spears.

PAUL Oh right, singer is she?

KELLY *(sarcastically)* No, she's a bus driver.

MRS RYAN Paul's a great fan of The Corrs.

PAUL Went to see them last year at the NEC in Birmingham.

LUCY I like the Corrs.

PAUL Yeah, and do you know how they got their name? Because every time they come on stage all the boys go 'COR'!

Lucy giggles, Kelly is not amused.

KELLY Oh, God!

MRS RYAN Anyway girls, you ought to be getting ready, the film starts at two.

KELLY That's all right, I'm not coming.

MRS RYAN What?

KELLY Jo's coming over and I've got loads of work to do for my History assignment.

MRS RYAN But Paul's bought the tickets for all of us.

Paul And a giant tub of popcorn.

Kelly Tough! I never asked him to.

Mrs Ryan Kelly!

Kelly *(sarcastically)* Enjoy the film. *(**Kelly** exits abruptly)*

Mrs Ryan Paul, I'm really sorry, I don't know what's got into her lately.

Paul Don't worry about it.

Scene Nineteen
Kelly's Room

*Kelly's room, a few minutes later. **Kelly** sits on her bed. **Mrs Ryan** knocks and enters.*

MRS RYAN Kelly, that was very rude.

KELLY I don't want to go to the pictures, I said so.

MRS RYAN I'm talking about Paul.

KELLY Oh, Paul. He thinks he can just walk into our lives with his cinema tickets and his popcorn and his pathetic little jokes.

MRS RYAN Paul's just a friend, that's all.

KELLY Oh yeah! And the rest.

MRS RYAN *(angry)* Kelly, I'm not sleeping with him if that's what you think! *(**Kelly** looks shocked and upset)* Look, I know it's not been easy for you since Dad and I split up but it's just as bad for me. Nobody wanted this to happen, we didn't plan it.

KELLY I know.

MRS RYAN No, I don't think you really do. *(sitting down beside **Kelly**)* Kelly, I've got to have a life of my own… there has to be some time for me in all this.

KELLY Mum, I realise that.

MRS RYAN No, hear me out. I can't change what's happened, I wish I could take the pain away for all of us but I can't. But it won't always be like this. You and Lucy have got your whole lives ahead of you… I mean, in a couple of years time you could be thinking of Uni… moving on.

KELLY Uni? I doubt it.

MRS RYAN You will and that's lovely, it's what I want for both of you but the point is, I'll still be here. Whatever you may think, Paul's a good friend, I like him a lot but we're not getting married next week. *(**Kelly** laughs weakly)* He's really supportive and he makes me laugh and, let's face it, I haven't had too much to laugh about in the last six months. I need a bit of fun in my life sometimes Kelly, don't spoil it for me.

Kelly *(tearful, hugs **Mrs Ryan**)* Oh Mum, I wanted him to be horrible but he's really nice. I do want you to be happy, you know that. But I can't get used to Dad not being here.

Mrs Ryan Kelly, our marriage may be over but you've still got a mum and you've still got a dad, and that's never going to change.

Kelly *(getting up)* I'm sorry, I'll come with you to the cinema.

Mrs Ryan No, it's all right, stay here if you want to, I understand. Besides, Jo's coming over.

Kelly I can see her tomorrow. I'm coming with you, right? Besides I love popcorn and I'm not letting Lucy scoff the lot.

Scene Twenty
Back to Earth

*Alan is sitting in the living room half-watching the TV and half-playing his electronic game. **Mrs Snow** enters quietly, watches him for a moment, then goes to sit nearby. **Alan** becomes aware of her presence and begins to lose his concentration on the game. He feels a little uneasy.*

MRS SNOW Alan, I... we need to talk.

Alan looks at her slightly surprised. Her tone is not as harsh as it has been lately.

ALAN OK. Have I... have I done something wrong?

MRS SNOW No, no, you haven't. Why should you think that?

ALAN Because whenever we talk, it's usually because I'm in trouble.

MRS SNOW Look sweetheart, I know that things haven't been easy for you lately. It's difficult between me and your father right now.

ALAN He used to be Dad, not father.

MRS SNOW Alan, it's me that's been doing things wrong. I haven't been as understanding as I should have been. *(**Alan** is surprised and a little embarrassed at this)* I'm apologising... to you.

ALAN Mum, what's happening to you and Dad?

MRS SNOW I don't know, sweetheart. Your father... I mean Dad and I just don't feel the same way about each other any more.

ALAN Why not?

MRS SNOW People just change sometimes and grow apart. Can you understand that?

ALAN Was it my fault?

Mrs Snow *(shocked)* Oh no, Alan! You mustn't think that, at all. What made you say such a thing?

Alan Because whenever you were arguing, it was about me; that Dad brought me home late, that you hadn't got me ready on time, that I was having problems at school.

Mrs Snow The arguments aren't about you, they're about us. It's a horrible thing to admit, but we just used you to get at each other. It was because of you that we stayed together for so long, but we just couldn't hold it together any more. I'm sorry, Alan. I'm so, so sorry.

Alan It's OK, Mum. You're both just scared. A friend told me that.

*Later in **Alan's** bedroom.*

Alan Hey Mary! OK, OK, I'll cut out the Mary stuff! I don't know if you're still there in my head, but if you are the weirdest thing just happened. Mum talked to me. She talked to me like Mum, and not some robot programmed for the destruction of her one and only child! I don't know why I'm feeling quite so cheerful – probably an unforeseen side-effect of that alien mind implant – or maybe it's just because Mum spoke to me like I was her son again. No, things won't ever be the same as they were. It's probably going to be cold war for some time to come. But then things won't always be like this. I can't see into the future, I haven't got the right equipment and my human brain is too minuscule. But maybe, just maybe, I'm heading in the right direction. This is Alan Snow, alien-friendly carbon life-form, astronaut-explorer to life's treacherous path signing out. Stardate twenty-six ninety-nine.

Scene Twenty-one
For Better for Worse

*Enter **Chorus**, including one couple dressed as **Bride** and **Groom**.*

CHORUS Lavender's blue, dilly-dilly, lavender's green
When I am King, dilly-dilly, you will be Queen
Lavender's green, dilly-dilly, lavender's blue,
When you love me, dilly-dilly, I will love you.

COUPLE For richer, for poorer,
For better, for worse,
Till death do us part.

***Bride** throws small plastic bouquet of flowers across the stage.*

CHILD ONE They went to war in 2004.
Mummy and Daddy are no more.

CHILD TWO So now things are not the same as they used to be.
Nothing can be the same again.
The world has shifted its axis.
Nobody shall reach the sun,
nobody shall touch the sun,
eyes will burn when they look at the sun.

CHILD THREE Mummy and Daddy, just people in a picture.
The frame is old, the glass is smeared.
Things are not clear,
but they're there,
two people in a picture,
together then – now apart.

CHILD FOUR Dear Mummy and Daddy,
the two of you made me,
but now there's only one.
You made me.
Let me wake up now –
let me be made again.

Chorus Lavender's blue, dilly-dilly, lavender's green… *(fade out. Chorus freezes)*

Enter **Kelly**. *She picks up the discarded bouquet of flowers.*

Kelly I don't think I'll ever get married. Well, not for a long time. I've learned my lesson well. And so now, here I am, Mummy and Daddy. You created me in your image. Then you moulded me to fit your games, both in need of a pawn, a party piece – a weapon. You gave me so many shapes that I forgot who I was. But I've constructed a new me, one that fits, a suit that I can wear. Like it? It's getting better all the time. I won't need to wear your love like a cheap cardigan any more. I've got me some body armour. So, shed no more tears for me. Like London buses, there'll be another like me along in a minute. *(looks towards the* **Chorus***)*

Chorus Sometimes arriving,
but always waiting,
waiting to disintegrate
or come together.

Staging the play

THE PERFORMANCE SPACE

Before putting on any play, you must consider carefully how you want to arrange your performance. The key is to be practical, flexible and imaginative in your approach. You need to be clear about what type of performance space you have before making any plans. Your space may be a proscenium stage, a classroom, or perhaps a very basic platform made up of stage blocks. Unless you know exactly how much space you have, it will be difficult to know where and how to position characters, props and other arrangements.

Remember that the director must always see things from the audience's point of view. Where will your audience be? In front of the stage? On all three sides? Or are you performing in the round, where the performance space is completely surrounded by the audience? The more audience you have around the performance space, the more you need to make sure that the actors are not blocking its view of the action. If you had a choice, where would you want your audience to be seated?

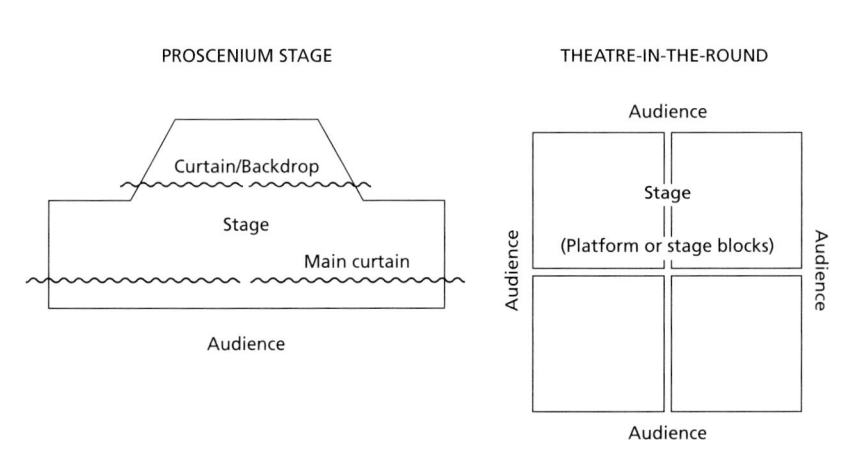

PROSCENIUM STAGE

Curtain/Backdrop

Stage

Main curtain

Audience

THEATRE-IN-THE-ROUND

Audience

Stage

(Platform or stage blocks)

Audience

Audience

Audience

Stage set-ups

SCENE CHANGES

There are a lot of scene changes in *You Made Me* as the action moves from one character's story-line to the next, and includes some Chorus scenes as well. A successful performance should be seamless. In other words, there should be a smooth flow, or transition, between the scenes, so that an audience isn't kept waiting for the play to continue.

How will you make sure that your play keeps moving at a suitable pace? Here are some tips:

- Avoid overloading the set with too many props and scenery, or they will have to be changed every time a scene changes.

- Sound effects can be used to set some scenes, which saves you from having to give visual clues. For example, when Alan and Mrs Snow are speaking to the Head of Year, the scene could be set at the beginning by the sound of a school bell and the sound of children walking, running and talking as they go to classes. When Wayne is in the car with Mr Northrop, the sound effect of traffic or a traffic jam could be used.

  27–28

  45–46

- Lighting is also very useful to indicate a change of location or to create a certain atmosphere. Through lighting, you can add to the emotion of the scene. For example, in Scene Three: Counselling, the children are all feeling uncomfortable and unsure of themselves and each other so bare, stark white lights might be used to highlight how vulnerable they are. A deep red flood for Scene Fifteen: Silent Scream where the Silent Child faces the Judge, could highlight the dark, nightmarish nature of her thoughts.

  10–14

  39–41

> ### ☺☻ Discussion
>
> **In groups** Consider how you would use lighting or sound to highlight the following emotions and scenes on stage. Think about what colours and sound effects would add to the dramatic effect you want to create. How bright or dark would you want the stage?
>
> - Anger
> - Loneliness
> - Madness
> - A summer's day
> - Scene Two: Words
> - Scene Seventeen: The Storming.

CHARACTERISATION

> 🗣️ **Discussion**
>
> **In groups** It is your job as an actor or director to bring the characters to life and to make them believable. Take each scene and decide what effect the writers were trying to create. What emotions did they want their characters to be feeling in that scene? Do the characters' emotions change as the scene progresses?

Anger

Anger is one of the key emotions in this play. All of the characters feel angry at the circumstances they are in, or at the way in which they have been treated. How do you, as a director or an actor, make sure that every scene is not acted in the same way? Think about the different ways that people show anger; it can be loud and aggressive, or soft and threatening (like Wayne); it can be intense but controlled (like Kelly); or it can come out in different forms, like the silence of the Silent Child or the Voice in Alan's head.

> 🗣️ **Discussion**
>
> **In groups** Give each person in your group a set of lines. Each person can then practise saying those lines, showing their anger in three different ways. Here are some lines you could use:
> - 'Sticks and stones may break my bones but words will shatter me to pieces.'   8
> - 'I won't need to wear your love like a cheap cardigan any more.'   54
> - 'Anger. That's all I know now, Dad. That's all I've got to get me through.'   46

Character development

Be careful not to allow the characters to become cardboard cut-outs or one-dimensional. Each of the characters, even Wayne, who is almost always angry, has another side. Try to portray each character as a real person, who is complex and can sometimes be contradictory. To do this you might need to consider how the characters develop through the course of the play.

> ✎ **Writing**
>
> **In pairs** Take one character and track their behaviour throughout the play. List the changes that occur. Using the list, write a monologue for the character, in which they show how they have developed and what they have become.

THE CHORUS

The Chorus has been a feature of drama since the theatres of ancient Greece. Originally, it was a group of speakers who recited the entire story in verse form. As time went on, the Chorus became less important than the actors who played the characters and acted out the story; by then the role of the Chorus was to break up the action of the play with either singing or verse.

What is the purpose of the Chorus in *You Made Me*? It is a vital part of the play, serving to put the events into a larger framework. The Chorus highlights the play's themes and contributes to its structure by appearing at the very beginning and again at the end of the play. It also provides an insight into the issues and sometimes speaks the thoughts and emotions of the characters.

The Chorus scenes are more ritualistic than realistic. The language used by the Chorus has a poetic feel and contrasts with the more natural speech used in other scenes. In production, the director and actors must think about how to bring the Chorus to life both visually and vocally. The way the lines are read needs to convey their poetry as well as the underlying emotions. The Chorus needs to work as a group and this presents opportunities to experiment with how the lines should be spoken. Here are several suggestions about ways in which you might speak the lines:

- The group might take alternate lines and speak a whole line each. One speaker might begin speaking a line and then another might take over halfway through, for example:

    Speaker 1: They went to war…

    Speaker 2:   …in 2004…

    Speaker 1: Mummy and Daddy…

    Speaker 2:   …are no more.

- Another effective sounding method is to echo lines or certain words; this gives the impression of depth and layering.
- One speaker could read an entire line and the others could come in on the key words.
- Breaking the line up into lots of parts can often give the Chorus impact; for example:

  Speaker 1: They…

  Speaker 2: …went…

  Speaker 3: …to…

  Speaker 4: …war…

  Speaker 5: …in…

  Speaker 6: …2004…

There are a multitude of ways in which to play the Chorus scenes but the best way forward is to investigate and experiment with an imaginative use of voices!

Drama

As a group

A. How would you present the Chorus on stage in a way that is different from the other characters? For example, you could use stage blocks of various heights, one for each member of the chorus. Brainstorm ideas for presentation.

B. Consider how the Chorus would speak its lines. The lines in the Chorus' scenes are poetic and abstract; they use parts of children's songs or rhymes and are often vividly descriptive. This contrasts with the earthy, 'natural' speech of some of the main characters. How can you make the most of the Chorus's lines?

THEMES AND SYMBOLISM

How could you design the set to show the play's themes, symbolically as well as literally? In the first counselling scene, for example, stark, white lighting could be used to highlight the vulnerability and separateness of the children. There would be chairs, since the scene is

10–14

set in the waiting room. Perhaps these could be set unnaturally far apart from each other, to emphasise the children's isolation from one another. Maybe Ros, the counsellor could be gaudily over-dressed to show how out of touch she is with the problems that these children are facing.

Isolation is one of the main themes and it is especially clear in the characters of Alan and the Silent Child. In some of their scenes, perhaps just a bare stage, a spotlight or suitable coloured lighting, and the character on their own would symbolise their loneliness.

Music and dance are useful tools to use if you want to work on symbolism. What songs or pieces of music do you know which might be relevant to the themes or would highlight the emotion of a scene? Think about whether a dance or movement sequence could be used to break up the scenes and to highlight the action. A stylised movement sequence could be used instead of a dance and may be particularly useful when thinking about how to approach the Chorus scenes with their stylised language.

Discussion

As a group

A. Consider the themes of the play:
- divorce and separation
- anger
- isolation
- helplessness
- uncertainty and vulnerability.

B. How might you use the stage to suggest these themes to an audience? Look at the following scenes and list your ideas.
- Scene Six: Piggy in the Middle (page 20)
- Scene Eight: The Commander (page 23)
- Scene Eleven: Fall Out (page 31).

Work on and around the script

THE CHARACTERS

Wayne
(See Scenes Three, Four, Five, Eleven and Seventeen.)

Anger and confusion are the two main emotions which Wayne experiences throughout the play. Consider Scene Seventeen: The Storming, his final scene in the play, in which he jumps out of the car. His parting words to Mr Northrop are 'Forget it Dad, I'll walk. I'll make my own way'.

Discussion

In groups

A. What do you think Wayne actually means by these lines? What has made him say this? How do you think an actor might deliver these lines?

B. Remember that these are Wayne's last words in the play.
- What are your feelings about how Wayne's story ends?
- Is it a satisfactory ending?
- Why do you think Wayne's story ended in such a way?
- How else might his story have ended?

Writing

On your own

A. Describe Wayne's final scene starting from his meeting with the Principal, Mrs Golding. Consider how the scene might turn out differently at the end.
- How might Wayne's attitude be different?
- What might happen between him and his father?

cont...

B. Wayne clearly has problems controlling his anger and this sometimes results in violence, like the incident with the Year 8 pupil. Devise a practical and imaginative self-help manual that would give someone like Wayne advice on how to control his/her anger. Remember that Wayne finds it very difficult to take advice or to listen to people.
- How would you catch his attention?
- What approach or design ideas could you use?
- How could the self-help manual be made to appeal to teenagers?

Kelly
(See Scenes Three, Six, Twelve, Eighteen, Nineteen and Twenty-one.)

Kelly's character is quite complex, as she experiences a mixture of different emotions based on her parents' separation.

Discussion

In pairs

A. Think about how Kelly feels she is treated and how she feels she ought to behave, especially towards her sister, Lucy.

B. What similarities and differences are there between Kelly and Wayne in the way that they handle their circumstances?

C. In Kelly's last speech, she says 'I've constructed a new me, one that fits, a suit that I can wear. Like it? It's getting better all the time... So, shed no more tears for me.'
- What do these final lines tell us about Kelly's character?
- How is this ending different to the ending of Wayne's story?
- Are there any similarities?

Writing

A. As a class Use a large sheet of paper or the board and write Kelly's name in the middle of it. Now brainstorm the range of emotions that she experiences in the play. Record your brainstorm in the form of a spider diagram.

cont...

> **B. On your own** Imagine Kelly ten years on from the end of the play, when she is 25 years old. Write an extract from her memoirs. It could include:
>
> - her reflections on her parents' separation and the events in the play
> - how things have now changed, particularly her relationship with her sister, Lucy
> - how her relationship with her mum's boyfriend has developed
> - how she feels about herself now that she is 25.
>
> **C. On your own** Kelly is very aware of how things should be and of how she would like things to be regarding herself, her family and her sister.
>
> - Devise a 'Wish List' for Kelly. This is a shopping list of things that she would want, to make her life perfect. It should include ideas on the way she would want things to be, as well as things for her own psychological and emotional well-being.
> - Now put together a 'Wish List' for yourself. What things do you want and need now? What do you want for the future? How do you want things to be different in your life? What do you want for the people who are closest to you?

Alan

(See Scenes Three, Eight, Nine, Fourteen, Sixteen and Twenty.)

Alan finds ways of coping with the break-up of his family through his vivid imagination. Unlike Wayne and Kelly, he is an only child.

> ### Discussion
>
> **As a class**
>
> - How does Alan cope psychologically with his traumatic situation? Do you think his way of handling the situation is effective?
> - How does the Voice in Alan's head treat him?
> - How does this relationship change through the course of the play?
> - What might the Voice represent?

✍ Writing

On your own Alan lives in a fantasy world, imagining himself as the Commander of Earth's Elite Defence Forces, battling alien invaders. Write the secret diary of Alan's imaginative life and call it 'Commander Alan's Confidential Star Log'. In it you should:

- build up a picture of the imaginary future world that Alan lives in
- show what role Alan plays in this make-believe world. Does he always triumph? What difficulties does he face?
- try to make his fantasy world reflect the events of his real world.

H

🎭 Role Play

In groups For a long time there is a great distance between Alan and his mother, Mrs Snow. They find it hard to talk to each other or to understand one another. Try a 'Thought-tracking' exercise.

Organisation You will need four people: Alan; Mrs Snow; someone to speak Alan's thoughts; and someone to speak Mrs Snow's thoughts.

Hold a conversation between Alan and his mother in which they don't say what they really want to, or they hide what they really mean. Every time Alan or Mrs Snow says something, the two people speaking their thoughts must try to say what their character is really thinking.

Situation For example:
- Waiting outside the Head of Year's office.
- After a counselling group meeting.
- After Alan's dad has dropped him back at his mum's house.

Opening lines For example:

ALAN	I'm sorry, Mum.
ALAN (**internal**)	I know she's going to be angry. I wish she'd understand.
MRS SNOW	As if I haven't got enough to worry about.
MRS SNOW (**internal**)	Oh no! I'm losing my temper again.

The Silent Child

(See Scenes Three, Fifteen and Sixteen.) There is only one scene in the whole play in which the Silent Child speaks and that is in a terrible daydream that she has during a counselling session. Like Alan, she lives an inner life that is hidden from the world.

Discussion

In pairs What effect do you think the Silent Child would have on an audience watching the play? What do you think an audience would think about this character who speaks in only one scene?

As a class
- Why do you think the nightmare courtroom scene is crucial to our understanding of the Silent Child? What does it reveal about her?
- How might a director try to make the nightmare court scene stand out from the rest of the play? Think about staging, lighting and sound. Remember that the court is imaginary.

In pairs Who is the Silent Child? Brainstorm what she might look like; what her home life is like; and what she might be thinking at various points in the play.

Read the poem 'A Boy's Head' on page 66. It is like a tour of the mind, showing its different aspects and the wonders of the imagination.

Discussion

The poem represents a boy's thoughts. What is in anyone's head tells us secrets about their character.

In pairs

A. Re-read the poem and make a list of what you think each of the things in the boy's head might tell us about him. For example: 'spaceship' = his wish to get far away from school.

B. List as many objects and things you think might be in Alan's head. Remember, certain objects represent certain feelings, thoughts and emotions: for example; an 'alien' in Alan's mind might represent his fears, or his feelings of being different to other children. Then sit facing your partner and take turns naming an object or thing which might be in Alan's mind and give your reasons why.

A Boy's Head

In it there is a space-ship
and a project
for doing away with piano lessons.

And there is
Noah's ark,
which shall be first.

And there is
an entirely new bird,
an entirely new hare,
an entirely new bumble-bee.

There is a river
that flows upwards.

There is a multiplication table.

There is anti-matter.

And it just cannot be trimmed.

I believe
that only what cannot be trimmed
is a head.

There is much promise
in the circumstance
that so many people have heads.

Miroslav Holub
Selected Poems of Miroslav Holub, (trans.)
Ian Milner and George Theiner, Penguin, (1967)

✍ Writing

On your own

A. Write a poem entitled 'The Silent Mind' which reveals the thoughts which run through the Silent Child's head. Look especially at Scenes Three, Fifteen and Sixteen.
- You can use the format of Miroslav Holub's poem to help you.
- Remember that the Silent Child probably has a very active imagination since all her thoughts are kept secret.
- You might want to start by drawing a head and labelling or drawing some of the things that might be in it (such as thoughts and feelings).

B. Write a poem called 'A Teenager's Head'. In it, try to explain what goes through the mind of a teenager you know.

C. We are told only a little about what has happened to the Silent Child and her parents. Write a series of four or five short scenes which tell this story and fill in the gaps about the Silent Child's background. There are certain questions you could answer:
- What happened to her parents? Why did they split up?
- What effect did that have on the family? How many brothers and sisters does she have?
- What kind of person was the Silent Child before she stopped talking?
- What caused the Silent Child to stop speaking? Was there a single event that made her go dumb, or was it a gradual build-up of things?

Themes in and around the play

MARRIAGE

In a typical wedding photograph, Greg Cordell and Carla Germaine smile for the camera on their special day. But this is a wedding with a difference. The couple won a competition organised by Birmingham's BRMB radio station to find two strangers prepared to marry without ever having met each other before! After the ceremony, which was filmed by Channel 4, the couple flew off to the Bahamas for a honeymoon paid for by a Sunday newspaper. They were also promised a year's free use of a luxury apartment in Birmingham's city centre and a Ford Puma car.

The happy couple

During the ceremony, the couple exchanged identical promises: "I commit myself to you and to our future life. I shall stand by you as lover and friend, whatever may come... I shall strive to love you for the rest of my life".

After the ceremony, the wedding was condemned by church leaders as a mockery of the sanctity of marriage. Callers to the radio station claimed it was a tacky competition and a waste of money that trivialised marriage.

Based on 'Nice to Marry You' by Sarah Chalmers, the *Daily Mail*, 26 January 1999

A few months after the ceremony, the couple announced their intention to split up. One of the reasons given for their separation was the pressure of the media.

By comparison, in the nineteenth century things were very different. Girls from wealthy families were rarely allowed out on their own and, when meeting a young man, they were nearly always supervised by a chaperone. A period of courtship before marriage could last many months or even years. A young person's choice of marriage partner was limited to those approved of by their parents.

> The etiquette of courtship was designed to protect the woman's reputation and hence her value in the marriage market. Hers was a purely passive role. To respond to a man's attentions before his intentions were known was to risk the ridicule of other people or the pain of disappointment. So she must appear hardly to notice, and certainly attach no significance to, male attentions until the moment of proposal…
>
> There was much behaviour prohibited to a young couple before they were engaged. This included using Christian names, unless connected by family; driving in carriages alone together; correspondence; exchanging gifts; and any kind of intimate touching.
>
> *Jane Austen's World*, Maggie Lane, Carlton Books (1996)

Victorian courtship

Now read the following extract from the *Daily Mail*. It looks at the predicted fall in the number of people getting married up until the year 2021.

> Figures taken from the Government Actuary's Department forecast that married people will be a minority just over a decade from now and that the young will not wed, divorce rates will rise but the number of couples living together will soar. Currently 55 per cent of those aged over 16 are married, compared to around 66 per cent 18 years ago.
>
> According to the projections, by 2011 only 47 per cent of women will be married and by 2021 only 44 per cent. By 2021, fewer than one in ten men under 30 and one in six women will be married.
>
> Over the same period the number of couples who live together will double from 1.56 million now to nearly three million, according to the analysis.
>
> In all, however, the Government Actuary estimates that fewer people will be living in couples and more will live alone.
>
> The actuaries reckon that by 2011, one in ten of all adults will have been divorced as against the present level of one in 12.
>
> These projections are based on trends in marriage, divorce and cohabitation.

Based on 'The Married Minority' by Steve Doughty, the *Daily Mail*, 9 January 1999

Discussion or Writing

In groups

A. Do you agree that the wedding competition on page 68 trivialises marriage?

B. Do you think that it is better to live together for a period of time before getting married? Explain your reasons.

C. Is it worth getting married at all in view of the rising number of divorces?

D. Organise a debate on the subject 'Marriage is an outdated institution and should be abolished'.

A proposal

Read the following extract from *Pride and Prejudice* by Jane Austen. In this scene, Elizabeth turns down a proposal of marriage from Mr Darcy.

Elizabeth felt herself growing more angry every moment; yet she tried to the utmost to speak with composure when she said, 'You are mistaken, Mr Darcy, if you suppose that the mode of your declaration affected me in any other way, than as it spared me the concern which I might have felt in refusing you, had you behaved in a more gentleman-like manner.'

She saw him start at this, but he said nothing, and she continued: 'You could not have made me the offer of your hand in any possible way that would have tempted me to accept it.'

Again his astonishment was obvious; and he looked at her with an expression of mingled incredulity and mortification. She went on:

'From the very beginning, from the first moment, I may almost say, of my acquaintance with you, your manners impressing me with the fullest belief of your arrogance, your conceit, and your selfish disdain on the feelings of others, were such as to form that groundwork of disapprobation, on which succeeding events have built so immovable a dislike; and I had not known you a month before I felt that you were the last man in the world whom I could ever be prevailed on to marry.'

'You have said quite enough, madam. I perfectly comprehend your feelings, and have now only to be ashamed of what my own have been. Forgive me for having taken up so much of your time, and accept my best wishes for your health and happiness.'

And with these words he hastily left the room, and Elizabeth heard him the next moment open the front door and quit the house. The tumult of her mind was now painfully great. She knew not how to support herself, and from actual weakness sat down and cried for half an hour.

🎭 Role Play

In pairs Read an extract from a teenage magazine that features a modern romance. Compare the language used in the extract above with that of the magazine. What are the similarities and differences between the styles? Try a role play that involves one person from the 19th century in a romantic scene with someone from modern times.

cont...

As a class Create a scene based on Victorian times in which a man is proposing to a woman in a middle- or upper-class household. You may wish to include the following feelings in your drama:
- shyness
- hesitancy
- bashfulness
- awkwardness
- embarrassment
- fear of rejection
- egoism.

Remember to apply the rules of courtship in Jane Austen's world.

Wedding vows

Read the extract from a Church of England marriage ceremony in the Alternative Service Book. The following words apply to both husband and wife who repeat them individually to the church, minister and congregation.

> Will you have [man's name] to be your husband? Will you love him, comfort him, honour and protect him, and, forsaking all others, be faithful to him as long as you both shall live?

Occasionally, a bride may also wish to include the original promise, from the 1662 Book of Common Prayer, to obey and serve her husband.

The couple also promise:

> To have and to hold,
> from this day forward;
> for better, for worse,
> for richer, for poorer,
> in sickness and in health,
> to love and to cherish,
> till death us do part,
> according to God's holy law,
> and this is my solemn vow.

⚭ Discussion

As a class Which of the lines on page 72 do you think are still relevant for couples today?

In pairs or groups of four Create your own marriage vows or promises for either a church wedding or a ceremony in a Register Office. Consider the following:

- obedience
- household responsibilities
- chores
- money
- equality
- cooking
- respect
- hobbies
- going out on your own
- children
- love and romance
- whether the marriage should be for life or limited to a contract of so many years.

✍ Writing

As a class Conduct a survey of your own class or year group.

- How many boys and girls hope to get married?
- How many do not want to get married?
- How many think it is a good idea to live with a partner before getting married?

Express the results either in graph form or as a percentage. Is there a marked difference between the attitudes of boys and girls according to your survey?

DESIGNER BABIES

The play shows how children both suffer and cope with the effects of divorce or separation within their family. It is obviously painful for everybody. What if it were possible to produce the ideal child who would not suffer in any way and would be able to adapt to constant change and the traumas of family life?

Cloning

Will there come a time when we will be able to order the perfect baby, selecting genes to produce the ideal choice in terms of skills, behaviour, intelligence, looks and the sex of the child? The evidence suggests that day is not far into the future.

Read the following extracts and look at the cartoon on page 77.

Could one man hold the key to life?

A beach bum turned scientist may be on the brink of discovering how to create artificial human beings in a laboratory.

Based on an article by Russell Miller, the *Mail on Sunday*, 9 May 1999

In the year 2525
Won't need no husband, won't need no wife
You pick your son, you pick your daughter too,
From the bottom of a long glass tube.

Lyrics from 'In the year 2525' by Zager and Evans

'Bokanovsky's Process is one of the major instruments of social stability!'

Major instruments of social stability.

Standard men and women; in uniform batches. The whole of a small factory staffed with the products of a single bokanovskified egg.

'Ninety-six identical twins working ninety-six identical machines!' The voice was almost tremulous with enthusiasm. 'You really know where you are. For the first time in history.' He quoted the planet motto. 'Community, Identity, Stability.' Grand words. 'If we could bokanovskify indefinitely the whole problem would be solved.'

Solved by standard Gammas, unvarying Deltas, uniform Epsilons. Millions of identical twins. The principle of mass production at last applied to biology.

'But alas,' the director shook his head, 'we *can't* bokanovskify indefinitely.'

Ninety-six seemed to be the limit; seventy-two a good average...

'For in nature it takes thirty years for two hundred eggs to reach maturity. But our business is to stabilize the population at this moment, here and now... '

Brave New World, Aldous Huxley, Granada (1932)

Most recent reports suggest that following the successful cloning of Dolly the Sheep, we may be close to cloning the first human being. Back in 1969, how remote that idea must have seemed when Zager and Evans recorded their song, 'In the Year 2525', confidently predicting designer babies but not for at least another 500 years.

Discussion

In pairs or groups

A. What would be the advantages of selecting or cloning children in the future?

B. Think about all the problems which might arise if society allows children to be created in this way. Consider:
- parents' wishes
- school
- occupations
- gender balance
- looks
- personality.

Both the lyrics from the song and the extract from *Brave New World* are predictions about how children will be raised in the future. But what is the main difference between them?

Writing

Imagine that you have travelled forward in time to the year 2525. Write an account of your adventures. You may wish to include the following information or paragraph headings:
- home,
- fashion,
- family,
- entertainment,
- transport,
- appearance.

✍️ Writing

On your own Look at the cartoon below. Imagine that you are able to create your own 'Perfect Parent'. EITHER design and label a diagram showing what they would be like, OR write an advertisement for one.

H

DR. SMITH'S CLONING CLINIC

EYES HAIR **PICK AND MIX**

BRAIN SEX

HEIGHT

So let's see, Mr. and Mrs. Jones, you've selected a boy, and you want the brains of Einstein, the face of Ronan Keating and David Beckham's legs.... Coming right up!

WHILE U WAIT

MONEY BACK GUARANTEE IF NOT SATISFIED

DIVORCE

Read the following extract.

Divorce 'a bigger danger than drugs to our children'

The breakdown of the family is a bigger threat to children than illegal drugs, according to the leader of Britain's schools, Mr Patrick Tobin. Addressing a conference, he claimed that rising levels of divorce and single parenthood damaged children by depriving them of the 'basic entitlement' of two loving parents.

Based on an article by Tony Halpin, the *Daily Mail*, 6 October 1998

This view is challenged by Jackie Anderson, President of the Girls' Schools Association, who claims that there are plenty of happy, well-adjusted people around who did not have the conventional two parents. 'Society should accept that children could be raised just as well in a broken home. Family, friends and neighbours can be a great support to a child. Divorce is a fact of life but damage limitation is possible if parents can be generous enough amidst their own hurt to ensure that the child is not divorced along with the partner.'

Based on 'Speaking up for Singles' by Tony Halpin, the *Daily Mail*, 17 November 1998

✿✿ Debate

As a class 'Every child is entitled to two parents as a basic right.'

Lisa, aged 16, describes her own experience of living in a one-parent family for most of her life.

> My dad left when I was about four; he used to travel on business a lot, but this time he never came back. I haven't seen him for 12 years. There is absolutely no communication between us. I never receive a birthday card nor a Christmas present, and yet I know he still lives in the area. Sometimes when I'm walking in the street I wonder if I ever pass him. I'm sure he wouldn't recognise me now. I do feel angry sometimes at the way in which he left us. It's like 'Why walk out of my life? What did I do wrong?' I think we have suffered financially over the years with him not being there. I've also spent a lot of time on my own. This experience has definitely made me a stronger person, but now I'm a teenager I'm very wary at the moment about forming close relationships with others. I suppose I'm scared about getting rejected again. Now I'm 16, I could make arrangements to see my dad again, but I feel if I did make contact it would be like letting my mum down. I know that if I saw him, I would be really angry with him for leaving us in the first place. There are so many missing years and it would be very difficult to adjust if he came back into my life again.

But for Tom, aged 14, the painful experience of separation was different.

> My parents split up two years ago. The arguing really affected me. I would be upstairs in my room covering my ears up so I couldn't hear them. Both Mum and Dad kept wanting to talk to me to explain their side but I couldn't handle this at all. At school I was really moody but I didn't want to talk to anyone about what was happening to me. In the end, it was a relief in a way when they did split up because then the arguing stopped. I still see both my parents regularly, they're happier now and talk to each other as friends. I wish they could get back together but it's not going to happen. I spend most weekends with my dad, which is good. Sometimes we go and watch Chelsea play if they're at home. I really like being with Dad but sometimes I still feel upset when I get in from school and I know he's not going to be there.

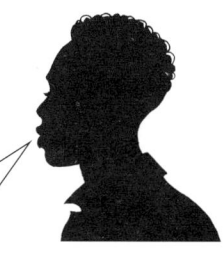

🎭 Role Play

A. In pairs Imagine a scene in which Lisa meets up with her father again after 12 years.

B. In threes Start an argument over any subject or issue. Allow a third person to come in between in an effort to cool things down. See if it is possible for the third person to reach a compromise with, or settle differences between the two people arguing.

C. In groups As parents, try and explain to your child (or children) why you can no longer go on living together and that you have decided to separate. This can be played with two, three or more people depending on the size of the imaginary family.

✍ Writing

On your own Who do you think suffered more from their parents' separation, Tom or Lisa? Explain your reasoning.

H

😊😊 Discussion

As a group What advantages does a child who lives with a single parent have?

Read the following extract from *Larry's Party* by Carol Shields.

As a landscape designer with projects across North America, Larry does quite a bit of traveling and he often sees divorce kids on planes. They're easy to spot. The flight attendant settles them in window seats and supplies them with crayons or puzzles before take-off, leaning over and speaking to them quietly as though to compensate for the emotional noise they've already suffered in their short lives. These children are clean and quietly dressed for the most part, with brushed hair and faces that wear the fixed breakable expression of accustomed but uneasy travelers. Nevertheless, they manage, despite their youth and anxiety, despite the brutalities they've undoubtedly survived, to project a sense of earnest sociability. They've done the trip before. A whole lot of times. Mom's in Texas. Dad's in Toronto. Or the other way around. No, they never get air sick (this said in prideful, yet shyly confessional tones.) They've been to Disneyland twice. They've seen the Blue Jays play. They're pretty good in Math, especially since Mom's boyfriend's been coaching them in division. As for Dad's girlfriend…

It tears at Larry's heart. It half-kills him!

Larry's Party, Carol Shields, Fourth Estate (1997)

Discussion

A. As a class How can you tell this extract was written by a north American author?

B. In groups What similarities are there between the description of divorced children in Larry's Party and the extract from the play (Scene Six) where Kelly is addressing the audience?

C. In pairs In what ways are children of divorced parents compensated for their situation according to this passage?

D. As a class Why do you think that the sight of the children 'tears at Larry's heart. It half-kills him!'?

Social trends

The graph below shows the number of first marriages, divorces and remarriages between 1961 and 1994 in the UK. Study the figures carefully.

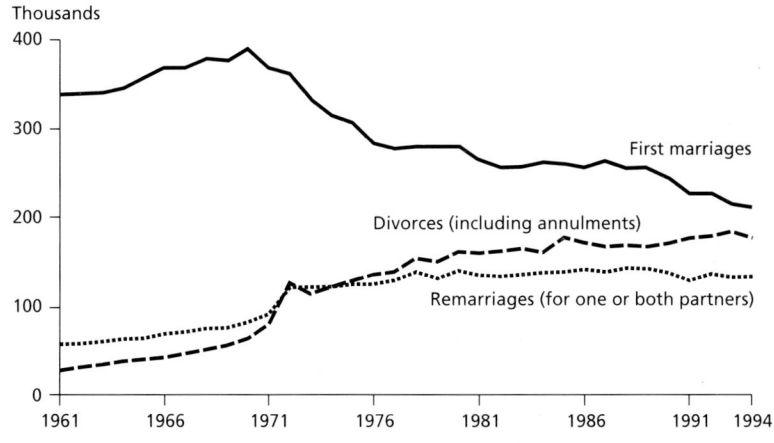

Marriages and divorces in the UK

Office for National Statistics

The graph on page 81 shows that the number of first marriages in the UK has decreased substantially since the 1960s. By contrast, the number of divorces has more than doubled during that same period. The Divorce Reform Act, which came into force in 1971, introduced a new ground for divorce, that of irretrievable breakdown of marriage.

Discussion

In pairs
- When do the figures for first marriages suddenly fall?
- What happens to the figures for divorces and remarriages in the early 1970s?
- What do you think that 'irretrievable breakdown of marriage' means?

Writing

A. On your own Copy out the graph but extend the time period from 1994 to the year 2050. Using different colours, extend the lines to predict how the figures for marriage and divorce will change.

B. In pairs Compare your graph with a partner and discuss the results.

Look at the table on page 83, which compares the number of divorces in countries belonging to the European Union. The figures are for 1994 and show the rate of divorce per 1,000 population.

Discussion

A. In pairs According to these figures, in which three countries are you most likely to be divorced? Where are you least likely to be divorced?

B. As a class In 1994, the Irish Republic did not permit couples to divorce. Do you think it would be a good idea if all countries banned divorce and insisted that couples stay married and work through their problems, perhaps with the help of trained counsellors?

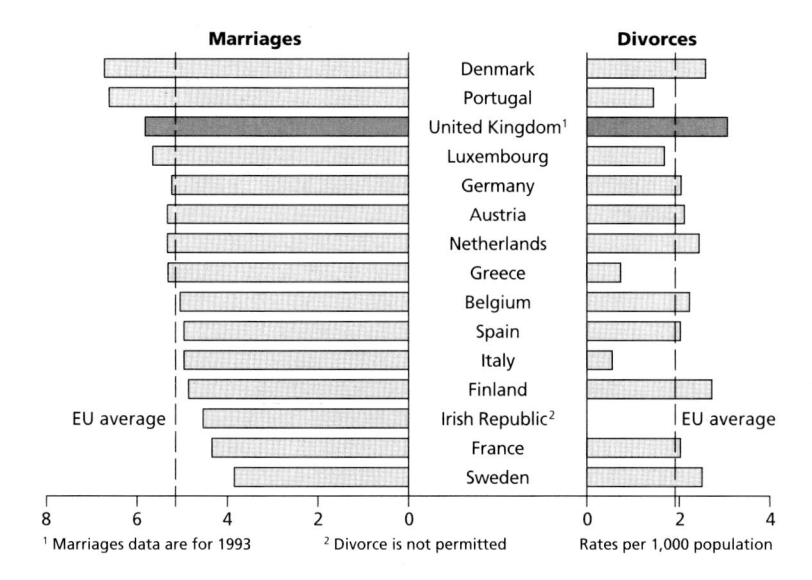

Marriage and divorce rates, EU comparison

Eurostat

✍ Writing

In pairs Look at the reasons given below to explain the figures in the graph and table. Discuss and write down the three most important reasons in your opinion which explain the large increases in the number of divorces.

- Couples don't regard marriage as a lifelong commitment any more.
- Not so many people get married in church these days.
- Life is more stressful, which causes more arguments.
- British women are more argumentative than Italian women.
- A divorce is much easier to obtain today.
- Children are causing more problems at home.
- Women are more independent and so don't rely as much on their husbands to support them.
- Divorce and separation are more acceptable in society today.

ISOLATION

Writing

On your own

A. Read Lucy's monologue, 'Situation Vacant', in Scene Thirteen: Long Division. Find up to ten words to describe her feelings at this point.

B. Imagine yourself in Lucy's situation. Create an advertisement for yourself, selling your good points. Draw and label five of your favourite possessions, either around the advertisement or on a separate sheet of paper.

C. Describe your most favourite possession and explain why it is so important to you. If you were forced to part with it for some reason, who would you give it to and why?

Scene Six in the play is called 'Piggy in the Middle' and many children often identify with this situation. They often feel guilty and blame themselves for problems in the home. The film *Parent Trap* shows children's desire to reunite their parents. Many children understand these feelings and wish for nothing more than to see their mum and dad back together again. Sadly, that is not always possible.

The following song, written by two, 14-year-old girls, expresses the feelings of many children in this situation.

On My Own

I'm sitting by this window
Hoping for my dreams
Wishing for a soul mate
To tell me what this means.

Chorus
I'm feeling lonely…

Why can't you understand
That my thoughts count as well?
I need someone to hold on to
To help me through this hell.

Repeat Chorus

Love's no longer united.
So many tears I've shed.
Which one of you am I to lose?
To end our love, I will not choose.

Repeat Chorus

Nicola Arthur and Georgia Dolenz

Writing

A. **In pairs or groups** Apart from the first line, the Chorus has been deliberately left out. Write another verse for the song and then complete the Chorus using either four or eight lines. In addition to the lyrics, you may like to try composing music for the song.

B. **On your own** Write your own poem, either beginning or ending with the following line taken from the play: 'You made me. Be careful. Handle with care.'

MEDIA

SOAPS

Read the following article.

HOW TV HAS HELPED DESTROY THE FAMILY

There can be few more graphic indicators of the traditional family's decline in modern Britain than the new format for the revived BBC game show, *Ask The Family*.

Where the contestants used to be restricted to married couples with their children, the BBC says that all types of entrants will be welcome, including single parents, uncles, stepfathers and perhaps even same-sex parents. The BBC claims its output has to act as a mirror of the new Britain. Society has changed since the programme started. The nuclear family is not as common as it was.

Soaps such as *Casualty* and *Eastenders* continually promote homosexuality while presenting family life as nothing more than a source of conflict, brutality and repression. As in *Eastenders*, *Brookside* gives an utterly negative picture of family life – so much so, that one of the few family-oriented characters, Max Farnham, is to be written out because he is too middle class.

Moreover, victim television such as *The Jerry Springer Show*, with its emphasis on dramatic and disordered private lives, tends to undermine the quiet routine of the family.

As one therapist said to me recently: 'Programmes like this are bringing deviant behaviour into the mainstream and giving it a dangerous appeal.' A happy, close, stable family has become a rarity of British TV. The message given out from a flood of programmes is that sexual experimentation and personal gratifications, not commitment and raising a family, are the keys to fulfilment.

The old virtues of sacrifice and concern for others are rarely heard. It is little wonder in this climate of hedonism, selfishness and alternative lifestyles that ordinary, traditional families should see themselves as boring rather than virtuous.

Based on 'How TV has helped destroy the family' by Leo McKinstry, the *Daily Mail*, 29 December 1998

There are many reasons why couples separate. It is very difficult to explain to other members of the family why this happens. Statistics show that divorce has increased rapidly over the last 20 years. Some people believe that the media, and television in particular, has encouraged the breakdown of family life because many programmes show marital affairs and constant conflict within relationships. Soap operas and chat shows are often blamed for portraying this in our homes on a daily basis. Read the article on page 86 carefully.

Discussion

As a class

A. *Eastenders… Coronation Street… Brookside… Emmerdale…* Is it true, as Leo McKinstry claims in his article 'How TV has helped destroy the family', that soaps only 'give an utterly negative picture of family life'?

B. Why are soaps so popular?

Writing

In pairs Do a survey of the most popular soaps watched by your class and produce a graph showing the results.

Research

On your own Concentrate on one soap. Over a period of a week or a month, log the number of one-parent families shown, compared to two-parent families in each episode, and note the number of characters involved in affairs with married men or women. Compare the results for each soap, then share your findings with the class. Is it true that the close, stable family has become unusual on British television?

In the article on page 86, the writer also attacks certain chat shows or 'victim television' such as *The Jerry Springer Show*, for undermining family life. Sallyann Keizer, produces and presents the Channel 5 television programme *The Mag*, which provides young people with the opportunity to discuss a wide range of issues. She outlines her views on what makes a good programme on pages 88–9.

CHAT SHOWS

Interview with Sallyann Keizer from *The Mag*

Q **Why are chat shows so popular with young people?**

A Young people want to know what others are thinking. Chat shows give them a chance to compare themselves with others. They are also assured that there are many others out there who share the same thoughts and feelings that they have.

Q **Why are some young people prepared to talk about emotional or personal issues in front of the cameras and a studio audience?**

A Sometimes it can be easier to discuss strong emotional feelings with strangers than with someone you are very close to. Many people quite enjoy letting go and talking about their personal problems openly, provided they feel secure and recognise that their problems are not being trivialised.

Q **Do you agree that television sometimes trivialises issues and exploits young people?**

A I think there is an immense danger that some programmes will sensationalise and exploit young people. At *The Mag* we do feel very strongly about this. We are very careful to be sensitive to the stories and situations of the young people on the show. My most important role is to ensure that young people are given a voice and an opportunity to tell their story within a secure and trusted environment.

Q **Surely the only value of such programmes is to entertain the audience?**

A The aim is both to inform and entertain. Young people gain so much from listening and watching others' personal accounts. They can change or modify their own opinions by listening to others and sharing their experiences through television.

Q **Do you think that chat shows can replace support groups and counselling centres?**

A No. Television can highlight issues but there will always be a need for back-up support. Peer-counselling has become popular today and it is important that young people have a direct place to go, somewhere accessible where they are given the opportunity to talk about their problems.

Q **What qualities or skills do you need to become the successful host of a television chat show?**

A This depends on the type of show and the audience you are trying to reach. I think that to work with teenagers you must have a genuine interest in young people and social issues. The most important quality is being able to listen. A good interviewer listens carefully to what is being said and then responds to what the person is saying. It is not a good idea to simply follow a list of questions. Some interviewers concentrate too much on the next question they are planning to ask without listening to the answers they are given. You also have to be aware of the studio audience, making sure that everybody has their say and that one person doesn't dominate the discussion. The presenter has to lead the audience and keep the discussion flowing, while facing the added distraction of the producer's voice in his or her earpiece giving instructions from the gallery. A good interviewer listens to what is being said and allows people to tell their side of the story.

🎭 Role Play

In groups Imagine that you are interviewing someone for the job of television presenter for a new children's programme. It may be a discussion programme, or it could involve sport, music or fashion.

- Prepare a few guidelines beforehand. Think about personality, work experience, communication skills, ability to listen.
- After the interview, you may like to try out the applicants' skills by asking them to introduce a link to the next programme, conduct a short interview with someone else, or read a news item.
- Each group can then record the full interview either on video- or audio-tape.

😊 😃 Setting up a chat show

In groups Consider the subject first and then the guests you will be inviting onto the show.

EITHER use actual characters from the play, such as Kelly, Wayne or Alan, perhaps projected five years into the future. The discussion could be based around the effects of their parents' separation on their lives. You may also like to bring in surprise guests by inventing new characters.

OR you may prefer to choose a completely different subject. The style of the programme might be an over-the-top or confrontational approach. Alternatively, you may favour a quieter debate style.

- Using the guidelines given by Sallyann Keizer, spend some time watching one or more chat shows. Decide who, in your opinion, is the best interviewer and write down your reasons.
- When recording, either using audio-tape or video camera, keep within a strict time limit (e.g. ten minutes) for the imaginary discussion programme. This would be helpful for the presenter, who will be trying to bring in all the guests and keep the discussion flowing.
- Each group plays back their recording and the rest of the class gives them a mark out of ten based on the following: the skill of the presenter; whether the programme informs as well as entertains.

Resources

Pride and Prejudice, Jane Austen, MacMillan (1982).

Pride and Prejudice video, BBC.

Selected Poems, Mirsolav Holub, (trans.) Ian Milner and George Theiner, Penguin (1967).

Brave New World, Aldous Huxley, Granada (1932).

Jane Austen's World, Maggie Lane, Carlton (1996).

Larry's Party, Carol Shields, Fourth Estate (1996).

Acknowledgements

The authors would like to thank the staff and pupils of Sawston Village College, Sawston, Cambridge, for all their help and support and especially members of the Creative Drama Group, who gave such a memorable first performance of 'You Made Me'. Special thanks also to Sallyann Keizer for her generous contribution to this book and her commitment to young people. Thanks to Susan Day for all her support and encouragement and for lending us Geri Halliwell's boots on two occasions for special performances! Thanks to Harriett Robins for voice-overs. Thanks to Susan Elkin for her encouraging review. Finally, thanks to Shane Reynolds for technical support and locating the virus that threatened to ruin the final disk one day before the deadline! We are very grateful to you all.

The following permissions to reproduce material are gratefully acknowledged: *Illustrations*: Nigel Jordan; p55; Gary Wing, p66; The *Daily Mail*, p68; Harry Venning, pp77, 84; Hulton Deutsch, p69; Telegraph Colour Library, p74; Bob Harvey, p75; Office of National Statistics, p81; Eurostat, p82; Sallyann Keizer, p88.

Text extracts: 'A Boy's Head' is taken from Selected Poems of Miroslav Holub, (translated by Ian Milner and George Theiner), Penguin, 1967, pp66; 'Nice to Marry You' is based on an article by Sarah Chalmers from the *Daily Mail*, 26 January 1999, p68; extract from Jane Austen's World by Maggie Lane, Carlton Books, 1996, p69; 'The Married Minority' is based on an article by Steve Doughty from the *Daily Mail*, 9 January 1999, p70; 'Does this man hold the key to all life?' by Russell Miller is based on an article from the *Mail on Sunday*, 9 May 1999, p74; Lyrics from *In the Year 2525* by Zager and Evans are reproduced with permission of Marvin Zolt, p74; extract from *Brave New World* by Aldous Huxley, Chatto and Windus, p75; 'Divorce "a bigger danger than drugs to our children"' is based on an article by Tony Halpin from the *Daily Mail*, 6 October 1998, p78; 'Speaking up for singles' is based on an article by Tony Halpin from the *Daily Mail*, 17 November 1998, p78; extract from *Larry's Party* by Carol Shields, Fourth Estate Ltd, 1997, pp80–81; 'On My Own', Nicola Arthur and Georgia Dolenz, p85; 'How TV has helped destroy the family' is based on an article by Leo McKinstry from the *Daily Mail*, 29 December 1998, p86; Interview with Sallyann Keizer from *The Mag* is reproduced with the permission of Channel 5, p88–9.